Alfred
Hitchcock

Serge Kaganski

Alfred
Hitchcock

POCKET  ARCHIVES

HAZAN

Cover illustration: Grace Kelly and James Stewart
in *Rear window*.

Page 87: photograph from Archive Photos, New York

© Éditions Hazan, Paris, 1997
Desing and production: Atalante
Documentation: Dominique Lebrun
Photoengraving: Seleoffset, Torino
Printing: Milanostampa, Farigliano

ISBN: 2 85025 531 9
Printed in Italy

Contents

Alfred Hitchcock died on April 29, 1980: sixteen years ago. And yet, like the heroine of *Vertigo* who comes back the Beyond, his name, his tubby silhouette, and the universe of his films continue to haunt the present. From the adventures of James Bond to the visions of Brian De Palma, filmmakers constantly recycle or restage the Master's inventions. The Gothic house and the shower from *Psycho*, the obsessive, lovelorn wanderings of *Vertigo*, the menacing feathered presences on a telephone wire in *The Birds*, the duel on Mount Rushmore in *North by Northwest*, the voyeurism of *Rear Window*, the sophisticated blondes in all these films, have become cinematic paradigms – eternal, founding figures of the collective imagination. Suspense is Hitchcock, just as dream theory is Freud, *la grandeur* is de Gaulle, purges are Stalin, home runs are DiMaggio, genius is Mozart, or Plans are Five-Year. The name Hitchcock has become a sort of trademark, even a term of everyday speech – like Frigidaire or Band-Aid. His name evokes mental images of the innocent and the guilty, of terror and of English humor, of elegant salons and sinister staircases, of breathless action and tormented romance – like an upsurge of the unconscious, a return of the repressed. Not bad for a director whose last shot went into the can more than twenty years ago. All the same, Hitchcockian clichés and visual flashes apart, who watches his films, who knows them, who remembers them? The young fans who throng to the films of Arnold Schwarzenegger, Brad Pitt, or Bruce Willis – do they have a memory? Do they know of the debt that *Dressed to Kill*, *Seven*, or *Twelve Monkeys* owe to the Old Master? Even to ask such questions is to suspect what the answers might be.

Son of a cockney

The Villains Always Get a Green Spotlight

Alfred Hitchcock was born on August 13, 1899, in Leytonstone, in the outer suburbs of London, not very far from the Cockney heartland of the East End. His father was a grocer and fishmonger; his grandfather was a policeman. There is no telling whether this grandfather had anything to do with his legendary fear of the constabulary, but there is one celebrated childhood anecdote. At the age of six or seven, young Alfred was sent to the local police station on an errand from his father. To tease the boy, or to teach him a lesson, the officer on duty put him behind bars for a few minutes, to show him what happened to children who did not behave. Whether this tale is true, totally false, or simply exaggerated does not really matter: what is revealing is that this was one of the few things Hitchcock ever said about his childhood. His police phobia is a thread that runs through his entire work. Contempt for uniforms, for the upper classes, and for authority and institutions in any form was characteristic of the Cockney society in which Hitchcock grew up, right on the borderline between proletariat and lower middle class.

Another dominant childhood concern, along with the police, was religion. The Hitchcocks were Catholics. This in itself was slightly out of the ordinary; and, as if that were not enough, young Alfred spent two years at a Jesuit school. Though mischievous and inclined to bend the rules wherever he could, Hitchcock was raised beneath a threefold yoke: that of a turn-of-the-century English upbringing, which by definition was rigid enough in itself; that of the Catholic religion, with its relatively strict moral code; and that of the harsh rules of a Jesuit institution. Fear of sin, and its inseparable concomitant, the desire to transgress, were in Hitchcock's blood as if by intravenous injection.

Young Alfred was a shy and solitary child, one of the few boys in his neighborhood who loathed sport and all physical activity. He preferred to stay in his tiny room and read rail schedules and books about trains. His father died in 1914, and at fifteen Hitchcock had to go to work to earn his keep and to help his family. He also started going out in the evenings and discovered the theater, its detective story lines, its comic devices, and its actors – some of whom later featured in his films. He learned one basic lesson from those evenings in the theater: the villains always get a green spotlight. Later, he became a moviegoer, discovering the numerous American films that were beginning to reach Europe. Buster Keaton, Mary Pickford, and above all D.W. Griffith delighted young Alfred and opened up a world beyond his previous imaginings.

He also read a great deal and developed a particular liking for Edgar Allan Poe, who taught him how pleasurable it can be to shiver with terror at a work of the imagination – especially from a safe and comfortable seat. Hitchcock was also excited by the work of Gustave Flaubert, and above all by *Madame Bovary*. He himself later declared that Emma Bovary – a woman who is destroyed by boredom and by a disastrous love affair – was his favorite character in fiction. Poe and Flaubert, terror and romance: as if by chance, the twin sources of Hitchcock's future art.

Big Alfred and Little Alma

After drifting from one temporary or menial job to another, Hitchcock wound up in an advertising agency, where he tried his hand at some short stories for the staff magazine. These reveal the strong influence of Poe, along with a partiality for black humor, a sense of the macabre, and a liking for farcical twists. In due course, Hitchcock found himself a job designing titles for Famous Players-Lasky, a subsidiary of Paramount, which had built studios in Islington, North London. There, not content with devising typographic or visual devices to make his titles more interesting, Hitchcock watched the activity in the studios, took an interest in all the technicalities of the business, talked with all the main staff directors, one of whom was George Fitzmaurice, and rapidly made his mark. Such a live wire was young Alfred that in 1923 he got his first real break, deputizing at short notice for the director of *Always Tell Your Wife*, who had fallen ill during shooting. This first effort had no immediate consequences, because Famous Players-Lasky began to wind down its operations. Caught between the audacities of the European cinema (Abel Gance, René Clair, the German Expressionist movement) and the power of the American movies under the leadership of Griffith, the British film industry did not pass muster, either artistically or – and this no doubt was the crucial factor in Famous Players-Lasky's strategic reappraisal – commercially. After a period of uncertainty and relative quiescence, Islington Studios were bought for a few pounds by a British producer, Michael Balcon. Hitchcock immediately redoubled his efforts, involved himself in everything, worked hard to get himself noticed, wrote scripts, worked relentlessly, and became one of the pillars of the Islington establishment. He did all of this to such good effect that in 1925 Balcon offered him a picture of his own for the first time: *The Pleasure Garden*, an exotic melodrama featuring the amorous entanglements of two couples.

Meanwhile, Hitchcock had become engaged to marry the studio's staff editor, Alma Reville, a girl as tiny and thin as Alfred was corpulent. They were married in 1926. Before he met Alma, it may be imagined that Alfred's sex life was very like the Illinois plains he showed in *North by Northwest*: desperately flat. The future, obsessional creator of *Vertigo* and *Marnie* had been raised by a remote, authoritarian father who had died before his time. He had grown into a solitary young man, sensitive about his appearance and his tendency to fat, so absorbed in his work that he had no time for courtship – or else so shy of girls that he chose to immerse himself in work. It is altogether possible that Hitchcock was still a virgin when he became engaged to Alma, at the age of twenty-five. There is a story about the filming of *The Pleasure Garden* that says a lot about the director's sexual experience. When an actress refused to film a scene in which she had to swim in the sea, Hitchcock's colleagues were reduced to doing a diagram for him: one year after getting engaged, and one year before getting married, Hitchcock still did not know about menstruation. His awkwardness in dealing with womankind in general (and with sexual matters in particular) is basic to any understanding of his creativity. It casts light on whole areas of his work: tormented romance, violent erotic impulses linked with terror and danger, a penchant for inaccessible blondes, frequently difficult relationships with actresses…

A Glass Floor

From *The Pleasure Garden* (1925) through *The Manxman* (1929), Alfred Hitchcock made nine feature films (rarely seen since their first release), which make up what is known as his silent period. During this first phase in his career, he was engaged in learning his trade, gaining confidence, and making a name for himself in the film world. These first nine films were often based on mediocre material: mountain melodrama (*The Mountain Eagle*), rustic comedy (*The Farmer's Wife*), popular stage plays of the day (*Downhill*, *Easy Virtue*). Routine though it was, this raw material offered him the chance to rise above the level of most contemporary British work by devising original camera angles and exploring the possibilities of lighting. Hitchcock was engaged on an artistic quest, strongly marked by German Expressionism; many Balcon productions were shot in Berlin studios, and the young Hitchcock soon found himself under the influence of G.W. Pabst and F.W. Murnau. Two films stand out during this silent period, both for their intrinsic quality and because they contain the seeds of work to come. *The Lodger, a Story of the London Fog* was described by its creator as "the first real Hitchcock picture." This story of a lodger whose landlady suspects him of murder is based on an eminently Hitchcockian theme: the innocent man unjustly accused, and the transfer of identity between innocent and guilty parties. In it, Hitchcock makes a point of devising purely visual narrative techniques. He films a young woman through a plate-glass window, lighting her from below to stress her blondness; and he installs a thick glass floor in the lodger's room, so that the audience can see his movements from the room below – a visual substitute for the sound of pacing feet, impossible to reproduce in a silent film. The theme and the oppressively Expressionist atmosphere, the foggy night scenes, the details of the landlady's daily life, build up a portrait of a society full of unease, a muted portrait of the ordinary people of London. Hailed by the critics, *The Lodger* was the film that first made the name of Hitchcock stand out amid the general mediocrity of the British film industry.

The Ring, in which two boxers compete for the love of a woman, is the "second true Hitchcock picture," according to its creator. The vicissitudes of love are symbolized by a bracelet in the form of a snake, which slips on and off the young woman's wrist and passes from one character to another... Hitchcock uses it as a visual device to symbolize an inextricable tangle of marriage, adultery, and sin.

Blood in the teacup

Ordinary People

Hitchcock's so-called British period runs from *Blackmail*, his first talkie, made in 1929, through *Jamaica Inn*, shot in 1939 on the eve of World War II. With the aid of sound and speech, Hitchcock expanded his repertoire of directorial devices, clarified the thematic and aesthetic lines of force within his work, and became an internationally famous director, celebrated as the "Master of Suspense."

The classic Hitchcock situation revolves around an innocent man who is presumed guilty. In *The Man Who Knew Too Much*, an English couple on vacation accidentally find themselves caught up in a case of espionage. In *The 39 Steps*, a young man finds himself having to dash from one end of Britain to the other, pursued both by Scotland Yard and by a secret organization. Aside from the obvious effectiveness of this as a dramatic device, Hitchcock may well have found it a cathartic release for his own fear of the police – and for the eminently Catholic idea that we are all potentially guilty. This pattern is reversed in *Sabotage*, in which the hunted criminal conceals himself behind the blameless exterior of a movie-house proprietor. (Did Hitchcock also mean that film is not really an innocent activity?) In *The Lady Vanishes*, a secret agent assumes the disguise of a respectable lady who looks as if she might play bridge with the Queen of England (and who shares that lady's preposterously antiquated dress sense). It will be seen that Hitchcock's characters are not supermen or Batman-type heroes but ordinary people, an assortment of representatives of the middle classes. The cunning Hitch knew all about audience identification: the best way to make a spectator respond is to put him or her up on the screen.

Fetishist Handcuffs
Another constant feature of Hitchcock's films is the way love emerges at the heart of the plot; the intricate interweaving of romance and danger in a relationship that crystallizes through action, often in the concrete form of a journey. In *The 39*

Steps, as also in *Young and Innocent*, a handsome young man drags a pretty girl into his adventure; in *The Man Who Knew Too Much*, a husband and wife are separated, find themselves in danger, and are brought together by their shared ordeal. For Hitchcock, as so often in his work, this characteristic structure has both a commercial and a personal dimension. As a professional who wanted to fill theaters, and as an instinctive practitioner of all the wiles of Hollywood, Hitchcock knew that he had to gauge and mix all kinds of ingredients; a touch of romantic spice enabled him to hold the female audience. It is also worth remembering that Alma Reville Hitchcock was not only the director's wife but also his closest collaborator. Alma had started out in films well before Alfred, and she had a superb command of editing, narrative structure, and other aspects of the craft. If she had not devoted herself body and soul to her husband's career, she might well have become a major filmmaker in her own right. Hitchcock worked in close collaboration with his wife, and he had a profound respect for her judgment – so much so that we may wonder whether his films might not have been idealized projections of their relationship. At an early stage in *The 39 Steps*, long before the hero and heroine fall in love with each other, they are handcuffed together. Quite apart from the tragicomic implications of such a situation, their relationship itself takes shape under constraint; it is as if Hitchcock were commenting on the nature of his own marriage – a contract sustained, maybe, more by professional ties than by any sexual and physical passion. Not that we can or should ignore the erotic fantasy implications of those handcuffs; Hitchcock himself admitted as much to François Truffaut.

Mr. MacGuffin, I Presume?

The dramatic energy in most of these films is generated by the celebrated technique of the MacGuffin. What is a MacGuffin? It is a false trail, a pretext, a goal that is vital only to the characters in the plot. We observe Hitchcock's heroes in hot pursuit of military secrets, scientific formulae, coded messages, about which the spectator really does not give a damn – and which, once revealed at the end of the film, often turn out to be a disappointment. The MacGuffin is to the Hitchcockian film what coal is to a locomotive: the fuel that keeps the action, the characters, and the audience running – toward the true objective, which is very much more like the attainment of a romantic ideal.

The journey counts for more than the destination. Hitchcock's movies are a perfect fit for Truffaut's suggested poetic definition of a film: a train hurtling into the night. Suspense in Hitchcock is not the terror of the unknown; nor is it the expectation of the solution to a riddle, as in the whodunit *à la* Agatha Christie. To make the most of the suspense, to be fully inside the picture, the audience has to be in the know. In *Sabotage*, Hitchcock very soon lets us guess the true identity of the terrorist; and, from that moment on, whenever the man appears on the screen, the tension is all the more powerful, because we know what he is really up to. When the saboteur hands a package containing a bomb to a child, the scene is terrifying for the spectator because he or she knows what the child does not know. In *The Lady Vanishes*, when the old lady disappears from view, we in the audience know that the heroine (who was on the train with her) is not insane, because we have seen them together. We are held in suspense, not by the issue of whether she has vanished, or whether the younger woman is deluded, but because we wonder who caused her disappearance, and how the heroine is going to prove herself both right and sane. In *Young and Innocent*, a children's party becomes the focus of tremendous tension, because the spectator knows that the hero and heroine, who are present, are wanted by the police. The tension is all the more acute because the party guests suspect nothing, and the hero and heroine are forced to behave as if nothing were amiss. Hitchcock knew that suspense was all the more effective when the audience knew what was at stake – and was better informed than some of the characters.

Brick Walls

Beyond all their adventure and romance, beyond their skill in catching the spectator's attention, the talking pictures of Hitchcock's British period are remarkable for their social background: like his earlier silents, they succeed in creating an image of a whole society. As already mentioned, Hitchcock's protagonists tend to be ordinary people who are neither superheroes nor (as in many Hollywood films of the same period) socialites. We meet detectives (*Blackmail*), working-class Irish people (*Juno and the Paycock*), average tourists (*The Man Who Knew Too Much*), a couple who run a small movie theater (*Sabotage*). What is more, these characters most often move in very ordinary surroundings, a long way from the lavish villas of Hitchcock's Hollywood period: brick tenements, tiny flats, crowded London streets, country farms, small shops, faceless crowds. Behind the mysteries of *The 39 Steps* or *The Lady Vanishes*, we glimpse between-the-wars Britain and the working and middle-class people among whom Hitchcock grew up.

The Limits of Insularity

Despite its imaginative achievements and its undoubted successes, Hitchcock's British period looks like a dry run for the American period. *The Man Who Knew Too Much*, *The 39 Steps*, and *The Lady Vanishes* still possess a certain dated charm, as quaint as the Britain of the 1930s; but the true masterpieces would all be made in America. Hitchcock's remake of *The Man Who Knew Too Much* outclassed the original; *The 39 Steps* became the immortal *North by Northwest*; and, when a lady "vanished" and reappeared in an American Hitchcock film, she had the carnal, lethal beauty of Kim Novak in *Vertigo*. (All these remakes suggest somehow that Hitchcock's career itself is structured like *Vertigo*, with its doubles and its reappearances.) Some of the reasons for this quantum leap seem very simple. In Hollywood, Hitchcock had more resources at his disposal, both materially – more money, better sets, better equipment, color, and the rest – and artistically: given an increasingly free hand, he was able to delve deep into his own impulses, his fantasies, and his unconscious. But there is probably another reason for the brilliance of the American period, a reason that seems obvious but is rarely mentioned: the actors. Hitchcock's Hollywood films featured stars like Cary Grant, James Stewart, Grace Kelly, Kim Novak, Sean Connery, Ingrid Bergman, Laurence Olivier, and James Mason. By comparison, Anny Ondra, Leslie Banks, Robert Donat, Margaret Lockwood, and Michael Redgrave were deficient in charisma, in fame, and in complexity. For all their undeniable qualities, these performers lend Hitchcock's British films a tone that seems too insular, too stereotyped, and insufficiently universal. The Master's contempt for actors is well known; what is less well known is that his prejudices derived from the behavior of certain English players. Britain is a country with a theatrical tradition, and for a long time the cinema was regarded as a popular entertainment, unworthy of respect. As a consequence, actors who came to pick up a fee in a film studio took their jobs very lightly, as a stopgap between one "serious" (i.e., stage)

role and the next. This casual approach, which
appalled Hitchcock, may well have played a de-
cisive part in his decision to cross the Atlantic.
He often wondered, he told Truffaut, why he had
never bothered to visit America before 1937.
World War II and a pressing invitation from David
O. Selznick gave him his cue.

Passport to Hollywood

With Measured Step

Hitchcock was initially slated to film the story
of *the Titanic*, but when that project ran into an
iceberg, somewhere in Selznick's teeming brain,
he turned to adapting Daphne du Maurier's no-
vel *Rebecca*. By a very Hitchcockian irony, his
first American film was thus to be an "English
movie": English subject and storyline; English
stars (Laurence Olivier, Joan Fontaine); a director who was straight off the boat from England
and still a total stranger to his adopted country.
If *Rebecca* had been made at Islington Studios,
would it have been the same film? Surely not.
Camera angles, music, sets, acting – everything
in *Rebecca* is ampler, clearer, grander, more evol-
ved than in the earlier films. The most striking
change in *Rebecca* is the total absence of the

celebrated, phlegmatic, poker-faced English sense of humor, which had always defused the inherent blackness of Hitchcock's message – like an urchin hooting with laughter after a cruel practical joke. In *Rebecca*, it is as if the émigré Hitchcock no longer has any fear of frightening the audience by unleashing his darkest impulses; as if he has freed himself from the British moral corset. Not one smile is permitted to relieve the tension. An eerie house full of dark corners, a haunting past, the intangible but obsessive presence of death: the tension never slackens from beginning to end. At one stroke the film becomes more credible, stronger, and more terrifying. *Rebecca* also contains a fine example of the way in which Hitchcock generated a climate of fear by specifically cinematic means: the character of the housekeeper. How does Mrs. Danvers terrorize Mrs. de Winter while doing practically nothing? First there is her appearance: dark clothing, dark hair, austere manner, forbidding features. Then there is the way Hitchcock directs her: all economy of movement. Still, straight as a die, her face severely impassive and her words few: everything about Mrs. Danvers is disturbing. Finally, there is her position in the shot: every time Joan Fontaine as Mrs. de Winter comes into a room, Mrs. Danvers is already there, like part of the furniture, as if she had been there even before Hitchcock called "Camera!" By her prior physical presence in the house and on the set, Mrs. Danvers jeopardizes the position of Mrs. de Winter, the newcomer, the outsider, who is not yet at home in her own "frame."

In 1941 Hitchcock made *Suspicion*, which is a sort of twin to *Rebecca*. It has the same English atmosphere (close to the Wuthering Heights romanticism of the last century), a plot centered on a couple separated by a growing sense of suspicion, and the same leading lady: Joan Fontaine, as frail and luminous as her surname suggests. The basic situation is simple: Lina, newly married to Johnny, suspects – wrongly, as it turns out – that he intends to murder her. Here, Hitchcock plays another variation on the theme of guilt changing places with innocence, but also suggests a vision of the man-woman relationship as the possible and indeed perfect locus of Evil. This vision is bolstered by a reflection on paranoia and the deceptive nature of appearances: Lina cultivates her fears by linking together unrelated facts, and by failing to communicate adequately with her husband. Hitchcock thus launched his American career with a pair of

David O. Selznick and Alfred Hitchcock, Hollywood, 1940

"English movies," as if approaching his new territory with measured steps – as if he first needed to prove his competence on familiar territory, and to acquire some power in Hollywood, before letting go completely.

Seen this way, the earliest of his films to be both a hundred per cent American and a hundred per cent Hitchcock – perhaps even his first masterpiece – is undoubtedly *Shadow of a Doubt*. Written jointly with the dramatist and Pulitzer Prizewinner Thornton Wilder, the film tells the ambiguous love story of a girl and her uncle. Brilliant, elegant, and charming, the uncle (Joseph Cotten) is really a murderer who has taken refuge from justice with a family of relatives who live in a small town "without a history." Hitchcock here reverses his perennial theme by wrapping a criminal in a respectable exterior. The fascination of *Shadow of a Doubt* lies in the way it unveils the ambiguities of human nature: the shadow side that exists in every one of us, even in the most brilliant minds. The film is also an absorbing portrait of small-town America. Long before David Lynch, Joe Dante, or John Carpenter, Hitchcock reveals that, beneath a peaceable, smiling exterior, America may conceal the vilest secrets, the most hideous grimaces. As a view of the U.S. by a recent "immigrant" – and thus a fresh and lucid view – *Shadow of a Doubt* is unusual among Hitchcock's American films in possessing a genuine social dimension inherited from his work in Britain.

Technical Challenges

In practically all of his pictures, Hitchcock was keen to explore the language of film and to devise purely cinematic techniques: there are numerous examples of this in his British work, from the transparent ceiling in *The Lodger* to the glass of milk lit from inside by a light-bulb in *Suspicion*, by way of the vertiginous tracking shot in *Young and Innocent* that sweeps the whole length of a ballroom to settle at last on the facial tic of the drummer in the band. Once in the U.S., Hitchcock pushed his confidence in the power of the cinema to the point of making entire films that revolved around technical challenges. Hitchcock set himself a challenge in almost all of his works; but in some he went further and embarked on a high-risk gamble. Thus, in *Lifeboat*, we are at sea in a lifeboat during World War II with a representative cross section of humanity, including a snobbish lady photographer, a nurse, an extreme right-wing industrialist, a religious

Black, an engineer, and a Nazi sailor. The film gambles on winning and keeping the audience's interest in this group of people trapped within the confines of an open boat, a little like the passengers in John Ford's *Stagecoach* – except that Ford's masterpiece also contains a journey, pauses, scenes outside the coach. In *Lifeboat*, we are confined to the boat, "imprisoned" in the vastness of the ocean for the entire length of the film. By surveying all of the intense feelings provoked by this situation, by bringing into play the moral conflicts and ethical issues posed by the presence of a Nazi (who also happens to be the only experienced sailor on board), Hitchcock makes his gamble pay off abundantly. One scene in itself sums up the director's ingenuity. As is well known, Hitchcock made a habit of appearing somewhere in each of his films – a kind of physical signature that leaves his mark indelibly on the film itself. But how was he to show up in an open boat in mid-ocean? Simple: on an advertisement for a slimming product, in an old newspaper left in the boat. *Lifeboat* is also distinguished by the intelligence of its message. When it first appeared, Hitchcock was much criticized for making the Nazi such a dominant and resourceful character. But if we regard the boat

as a symbol of the Earth, with its passengers acting out the geopolitical situation, the metaphor
of *Lifeboat* is irrefutable. At the time when the
film was made, in 1943, the Nazis had taken ad-
vantage of the weakness and disorganization of
the democracies and had taken the helm of world
affairs. Contrary to the criticisms leveled at him
by the "politically correct" circles of the time,
Hitchcock was not making the Nazis look better
than they were; he was just telling the American
public the truth. No doubt he felt some guilt
about peacefully carrying on with his career, while
London was being pounded to ruins by the
German bombs. And so *Lifeboat*, along with
Foreign Correspondent, may be considered as his
contribution to the British war effort – apart, that
is, from the two anti-Pétain shorts he made for
the Ministry of Information in Britain in 1944.
The artistic and technical challenge of *Rope* is a
time-honored cinematic Great White Whale: a
film that is shot in one unbroken sequence, without cuts or joins, freed from editing and all the
trickery that goes with it; the cinematic ideal of
a single shot/sequence, recording the story in all
its fluid continuity – and equating with the "seam-
less reality" so dear to the heart of André Bazin.
As each reel of film plays for just ten minutes,

Hitchcock needed to get around the necessary
transitions: he contrived to end and begin every
reel with the camera trained on a close-up of furniture or clothing that would make the joins
invisible.

Making this film look like a "single shot" and
play in real time (the duration of the action being
identical with that of the projection) was undoubtedly a headache for the entire production
team, most notably the set decorators, the prop-
erty staff, and the continuity girl. More than in
any other film, there had to be total continuity
between shots in such matters as the positions
of the furniture and of the actors (the "single
shot" being of course an illusion). As the action
of *Rope* takes place in the course of one evening,
it was necessary to make a credible transition
from afternoon light to twilight and then to
night. The film is mainly set in a living room lit
by an immense window; Hitchcock paid careful
attention to the movement of the artificial clouds
in the studio sky that is seen in the background
throughout the film. The best thing about *Rope*
is that we soon forget the technical and aesthetic challenge: the film holds us by its suspense,
by its macabre irony (a corpse is hidden in a trunk
in the middle of the room, and the unsuspecting

guests calmly converse around it), and by its debate on the issues of crime and guilt. As a contribution to film theory, *Rope* has had few successors. Ironically enough, this film shot in a "continuous take" may well have required more manipulations, adjustments, directorial devices, and pieces of trickery than conventionally "edited" films. Many films since have emphasized the fluidity of the single shot that turns into a sequence; there have been some shorts made in one shot (including Jean Rouch's segment of *Paris*, *vu par…*); but no feature film has been based on the principles of *Rope*. Nevertheless, *Rope* was well worth trying. It remains a fascinating artistic experiment, a unique object, and at the same time a tangible proof of the infinite possibilities of film.

Dial M for Murder rests, like *Rope*, on an longstanding technical ambition: in this case the rendering of three dimensions. However, like the single-shot technique of *Rope*, the 3-D of *Dial M* never went beyond isolated experiments to become a widely used technique. It beautifully underscores several effects in the film (a telephone dial in close-up, a pair of scissors emerging from the screen to flirt "dangerously" with the spectator's nose), but it has to be admitted that this very English mystery story, with its phlegmatic detective, can perfectly well be seen in its standard version. The 3-D process is ultimately uninteresting, for several reasons. It demands a rather complicated technical infrastructure (special projectors, glasses to be given out to the audience), and it starts to get very tiring for the eyes after a quarter of an hour or so. Above all, three-dimensional form in cinema is pointless – even pleonastic – because the third dimension is already there, in the depth of field and in the tracking shots that make it possible to hollow out the surface of the screen. The third dimension is created in the eye and in the brain, as the spectator "projects" into the film his or her own fantasies, thoughts, and reactions. It is this constant circulatory process linking the screen with the spectator, this matching of filmic images with mental images, that constitutes true depth in cinema. So clearly did Hitchcock perceive this that he went on to create masterpieces that were metaphors in themselves of the relationship between film and spectator: works endowed with a material presence, a density, and a relief quality that rendered the 3-D process utterly dispensable and obsolete.

Cinematic Depths

Of all Hitchcock's films, it is *Rear Window* that most lucidly outlines an allegory of cinema. James Stewart plays a press photographer laid up at home with a broken leg; condemned to idleness, he spends most of his time looking out at the courtyard behind his apartment block, watching the windows opposite and the comings and goings of his neighbors, both in the yard and in their homes. As he does so, he comes to the conclusion that he has uncovered a murder in one of the apartments. Aside from the suspense of the murder story and the view of a slice of urban life, the coded message of *Rear Window* is pretty clear: the building opposite is a movie screen – or rather, each window is a separate screen. Immobilized in his chair, the Stewart character is at once the spectator, the projectionist, and the director. For the first third of the action he remains the spectator, doing nothing but observe passively; in the second third he becomes the projectionist, when he observes a row between husband and wife, followed by curious comings and goings on the part of the suspect, and begins to "project" his murder story. Watching the windows opposite, Stewart the spectator can see only a silent film and fragments of images: the gaps, the rows of dots, the missing images, and the dialogue are supplied by his brain – aided and abetted by his fiancée/nurse, graciously played by the future Princess Grace. Since the Stewart character is a man of the image and a man of action, paralyzed by his injury, it is perfectly logical for him to adopt the active role of director in the final third of the picture. By sending Kelly to the suspect's apartment, he directs and intervenes: by overstepping the divide between his position and the private life of his neighbors, he crosses the frontier between auditorium and screen, between spectator and director. It is Hitchcock's supremely elegant achievement to have inserted this remarkable reflection on film, and on the relationships between the creator, the work and the spectator, into an exciting and universally comprehensible story. It is part and parcel of Hitchcock's genius that he is able to speak both to the Saturday-night audience and to the most ingenious scholarly interpreters; and the most remarkable common feature of his masterpieces is that they satisfy commercial criteria just as well as they satisfy the loftiest artistic demands.

North by Northwest is the classic case of a film made to be read on multiple levels. Regarded as an American remake of *The 39 Steps*, it is incomparably superior to its original in brilliance, beauty, and density. This story of an ordinary American caught up against his will in a grim case of espionage is, once more, the story of the spectator who becomes the protagonist of his own film. In *Rear Window*, Stewart stayed put in his wheelchair, at a distance from the wall/screen; when he intervened, he did so without moving, by remote control, by sending someone else down onto the "studio floor." In *North by Northwest*, Cary Grant is in a precisely opposite situation: far from being immobilized, he is all over the place, gesturing, running, chasing over hill and dale. He is like a spectator who jumps out of his seat and walks into the screen; a spectator who becomes the hero of the film. That remarkable critic, Jean Douchet, takes this view of things much further. In his interpretation, Grant represents the Audience, Eva Marie Saint represents the Work of Art, James Mason is the suicidal aspect of the Artist, the spy chief stands for the commercial concerns of the Director, and Mason's attendant thug is the Critic. While Douchet's analysis is particularly convincing – revealing as it does an additional dimension of genius in *North by Northwest* – it remains to be said that this film

also embodies a hypothesis concerning the function of art itself: namely, that art is something
that serves to fill a void. *North by Northwest* is
founded on a principle directly opposed to that
of *The Lady Vanishes*. In the British picture, a real
spy falsely assumes the appearance of a vener-
able lady removed from view by rival spies. In
North by Northwest, Grant is a real Mr. Everyman
who serves to fill the empty shell of a totally fic-
titious spy; he lends shape to a decoy. It is not
that the lady vanishes, but that the man appears.
This image of a void that has to be filled is perfectly summed up in the celebrated sequence
that begins with a desperately flat, empty plain
– a blank page that is then "filled" by the presence of the hero and of a crop-dusting aircraft.
North by Northwest thus perfectly illustrates the
time-honored MacGuffin principle: the characters and the spectators are pursuing an objective
(espionage secrets) that is no more than a pretext: what counts is the chase, the journey,
keeping the screen filled – and filled to some effect. Both for the characters and for the audience,
there is another ultimate objective: the amorous
union between Grant and Saint. As so often in
Hitchcock, espionage is no more than a plot en-
gine that sets off a process basic to his work: the

birth of love and the crystallization of a relationship. Who knows? Maybe the portly director made his MacGuffin films in the secret hope of winning those blonde stars of his when shooting ended? A hope eternally disappointed and therefore eternally renewed.

Seen in this light, *Vertigo* is perhaps the absolute Hitchcockian masterpiece, a parable of the cinema and of the inmost recesses of its creator's soul. Organized in terms of duality (two women, and a narrative in two parts), the structure of *Vertigo* reflects the dual, reversible essence of cinema: negative/positive, exposure/development, shooting/projection. In the first part, James Stewart pursues Kim Novak and falls madly in love with her. The energy circulates from Novak to Stewart; she has a drastic effect on him, but he has no effect on her. Stewart is like a camera (or like unexposed film stock), "imprinted" with Novak's image. In the second part, this process is reversed. Stewart is trying to transform Novak 2 into the exact image of Novak 1. This time, the energy flows from Stewart to Novak; he has an effect on her, and it is she who is passive, as if Stewart the camera/film had now become a projector. Stewart projects onto Novak 2 the pre-recorded image of Novak 1. After *Rear Window* and *North by Northwest*, *Vertigo* concludes a royal trilogy on the Seventh Art. Above all, however, *Vertigo* remains one of the most romantic, sensual, dreamlike films in the history of the cinema, a harrowing poem of love, an obsessive, desperate erotic fantasy – which brings us to the crux of Hitchcock's work, the deepest part of the director's psyche.

The Law of Desire

As Hitchcock's career progressed, his art grew richer and more profound. On a technical level, he became an unquestioned master of the art of manipulating an audience; at the same time his films became more complex and more personal, culminating in the richness of *Psycho* and *The Birds* and the intimate depth of *Vertigo* and *Marnie*. By this time, the director was no longer merely playing with his audience, amusing it or scaring it; he was exploring the dizzying depths of his own soul. Behind the adventure, the romance, and the suspense lurks a harrowing confessional message.

Phonetically – though not many people seem to have noticed the fact – the name Hitchcock is very like "itch cock." The argument may seem hazy, but even so: Hitchcock was a virgin when he married, and he lived for the rest of his life. in a marriage which was stormy at times, and which was primarily based on a strong professional relationship. Alongside that marriage, Hitchcock spent his time filming the most beautiful creatures: cool, aloof blondes, who seem to have represented a supreme ideal for this short, obese, dark, bald man. Hitchcock directed them, ordered them around, manipulated them, spied on them, "undressed" them with the camera lens – but never dared, or was never able, to put his arms around them. Maybe Hitchcock's life story can be reduced to this: a man obsessed, frustrated, repressed, to whom sex was a constant itch, and who – unable to satisfy his desire – transcended himself in his creative work. It was his achievement to transform this neurotic state of affairs into film for our benefit. Seen thus, *Vertigo* is a classic symptom of Hitchcock's malady: the story of a man madly in love, obsessed by a woman to the point of trying to bring her back from the dead. In the James Stewart character, who obsessively acts out the role of Pygmalion, compulsively adjusting every last detail of his "work of art," we can but recognize Hitchcock himself, molding his actresses, composing his films with extraordinary care.

With *Psycho*, the first psychoanalytical thriller, Hitchcock digs even deeper into the labyrinth of his and our unconscious. It has already been pointed out how amazingly modern *Psycho* is: it starts with illicit sex, continues with a theft, a dash across the Arizona desert that is like a bad dream, and leads up to the famous and terrifying shower scene in which the central character is eliminated – all this in the first quarter of the film. Seeing *Psycho* again now, we begin to understand the way in which the shower scene is both feared and desired: Hitchcock may be scaring his female viewers out of their wits, but he is turning his male viewers into potential rapists, since Janet Leigh has been turning men on ever since she appeared in her brassiere in the first scene. Aside from its cathartic function, directed at the male viewer, the shower killing may have several meanings. Perhaps Norman Bates is trying to eliminate a dangerous rival to his "mother"? Might this also be, for Hitchcock, a perverse plot mechanism, a drastic way of trading one principal character in for another? Leigh has served her purpose; the film no longer needs her; out she goes. If Anthony Perkins is to take the heroine's place at the centre of *Psycho*, he will have to murder her first. The

Alfred Hitchcock with Bernard Herrmann, who composed the music for many of his films, on the set of *Vertigo*, 1958

places in *Psycho* are fundamental: the deserted motel, the famous Gothic house on the hill, its staircase, its cellar, the amniotic swamp into which the victims are plunged… it all sends us straight back to psychoanalysis, and to the different levels of consciousness within the fractured brain of Norman Bates. In this brutal, violent, and (by the standards of the major Hollywood productions of the time) bizarre picture, Hitchcock puts on the table what was already latent in his earlier films: the elemental, sexual, murderous impulses within a human being. *Psycho* is an untamed, unmannerly film; only its explanatory ending has dated. Beneath the distinguished, well-fed, jovial exterior of an English prankster, Hitchcock was a damaged man – a seething mass of desires and frustrations that were to boil over in the two films that followed.

The Birds and *Marnie* may not be the best pictures Hitchcock ever made (though even that is debatable), but they are certainly key sources for anyone who seeks to catch sight of the links between the director's private life and his work. The key is to be found in one name: that of Tippi Hedren. No doubt she was not the only actress Hitchcock ever fell for, but she was the only one to whom he made an open declaration of love.

Today, on revisiting *The Birds*, that masterpiece of pure, primitive terror, we begin to sense that Hitchcock made it for one reason and for one reason only: to abuse Tippi Hedren, to scare her, to give her a hard time, to push her to the edge, to lacerate those pellucid features, to spoil that maddening beauty. It seems like the work of a sadist who so resents his position of emotional inferiority to his own star that he goes out of his way to assail and humiliate her – a backhanded way, to put it mildly, of declaring his love.

It all came to a head during the shooting of *Marnie*. In desperation, he told Hedren he loved her, clumsily paid court to her, and suffered a painful rebuff. Hitchcock was a broken man; *Marnie* was completed in a dense cloud of muddle and ill-feeling; and Hedren's career came to an abrupt end. *Marnie* now looks like a low-rent version of *Vertigo*, a spoiled masterwork – what Truffaut used to call *un beau film malade*, a good movie in bad health. It looks, in fact, like a metaphor of its own making. *Marnie* is the story of a frigid woman who obstinately refuses herself to her husband; the parallel with Hitchcock's relationship with Hedren could hardly be clearer. The opening shot is masterly: a close-up of a handbag, its pleat as crucial as the spiral of Novak's

chignon in *Vertigo*. That pleat does look terribly
like a hole, a crack – but the purse is firmly fast-
ened, gripped under Marnie's arm. Marnie is a
kleptomaniac, and the picture has more keys in
it than *a roman à clef*. In the office of her new
employer, Marnie sets out to get hold of the key
of a drawer that contains the combination to the
safe. She succeeds in abstracting the key, then
the combination, then the money. The employer
catches her out, confronts her, desires her – and
spends the rest of the film doing just what she
has been doing: trying to find the (psychoanal-
ytic) combination that will enable him to open
up Marnie's legs and her mind, which are lock-
ed fast against him, like a strongbox.
Vertigo, *Psycho*, and *Marnie* frequently resemble
dreams; they flirt with a dream quality so powerful that it carries the spectator far away from
the real world and into an extraordinary realm
"projected" from the director's tormented brain.
At the outset of his monumental biography of
Hitchcock, Daniel Spoto remarks that he has little
first-hand information to go on: throughout
his career, the maker of *Psycho* was discreet about
his private life, almost invariably handing out the
same anecdotes, the same stories, the same jokes,
the same smokescreen concealing a profounder

truth. What Spoto fails to realize is that Hitchcock's inner life is all there inside his films, and that the resulting body of work is worth a hundred true confessions. Comic, harrowing, inventive, rich in suspense, superbly crafted: Hitchcock's films certainly are all these things. But there is far more to them than that. To borrow an expression of Serge Daney's, they are his unconscious mind, brought out into the open.

Hitch Lives

After *Marnie* and its backstage agonies, Hitchcock's creative impulse seemed to have been broken. None of his four last films was to attain the heights of *Vertigo* or *Psycho*. The Master used his own formulas a little mechanically (*Torn Curtain*, *Topaz*); made a pleasing return to London with *Frenzy*, which revives the macabre humor of his British period; and ended with a rather lame and breathless curiosity, *Family Plot* – which Jean Douchet, ever the individualist, regards as his final masterpiece, an artistic testament combining every facet of Hitchcock's work. Old age, and rejection by Tippi Hedren, had vanquished his genius. Even though there has been no space to discuss such great *films malades* as *Under Capricorn*, or such curiosities as *The Trouble with Harry*, or even such

Alfred Hitchcock and François Truffaut

masterpieces as *Notorious*, *Strangers on a Train*, or
the remake of *The Man Who Knew Too Much*, it
is essential at this point to take a look at Hitchcock's
posthumous existence, and at his influence on
contemporary film – starting out with his New
Wave admirers in France, notably Truffaut and
Claude Chabrol. Hitchcock's inquiry into the nature of Evil, his black humor, his symbolic use
of a house or a precise location, are persistent
threads in Chabrol's work: *Le Boucher*, *La Femme
infidèle*, *L'Enfer*, and the recent *La Cérémonie* are
striking examples. Truffaut was influenced above
all by the romance and the subliminal erotic power of Hitchcock's films; in this tormented vein,
Les Deux Anglaises, *Adèle H*, and *La Femme d'à
côté* are siblings to *Notorious*, *Under Capricorn*,
and *Vertigo*. Truffaut also worked with Bernard
Herrmann, whose music is inseparable from
Hitchcock's world. Brian De Palma was so strongly influenced by Hitchcock that he was long
mistaken for a mere imitator without any resources of his own. *Carrie* and *Dressed to Kill*
incorporate both thematic and structural ele-
ments from Hitchcock's work, including the
shower scene from *Psycho*, which reappears several times in each film. A work like *Body Double*
is like a collage of *Vertigo* and *Rear Window*. This

said, De Palma has often introduced his own obsessions into the Hitchcockian framework; and, as he has demonstrated, he is quite capable of making films that owe little to Hitchcock's example (*The Untouchables*, *Casualties of War*, *Carlito's Way*). The whole James Bond series is based on a framework lifted more or less straight from the storyline of *The 39 Steps* and *North by Northwest* – though the likable 007 goes for the dry bones of Hitchcock and has no inkling of the true essence (which in any case is presumably not what the producers of the series have in mind). *The Colombo* detective series seems to be inspired by Hitchcock's "chamber-music" films, notably *Dial M for Murder* – whose French title, literally "The Crime Was Almost Perfect," might serve for any episode in the series. A film like *Twelve Monkeys*, by Terry Gilliam, is full of lessons learned from Hitchcock – so much so that it includes a quotation from *Vertigo* and has its two lead characters hide in a cinema that is showing a Hitchcock festival! Truth to tell, there is probably a whiff of Hitchcock in eighty per cent of American action pictures. Hitchcock so permeated, mastered, possessed, and loved the cinema that today, more than sixteen years after his death, he is more alive than ever.

The Early
Films

Alfred Hitchcock and his wife the script writer Alma Reville, Hollywood, 1940
Hitchcock filming in England in the thirties

Gordon Harker and Carl Brisson in *The Ring*, 1927

Anny Ondra in *Chantage*, 1929

Leon M. Lion and Anne Grey in *Number Seventeen*, 1932

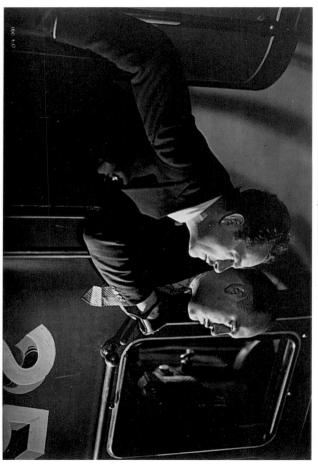

Donald Calthrop in *Number Seventeen*, 1932

Esme Percy and Herbert Marshall in *Murder*, 1930

The American poster for *The Man Who Knew Too Much*, 1934

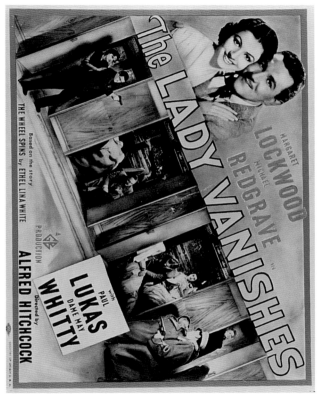

Passengers of the train in *The Lady Vanishes*, 1938

Charles Laughton, Maureen O'Hara and Robert Newton in *Jamaica Inn*, 1939

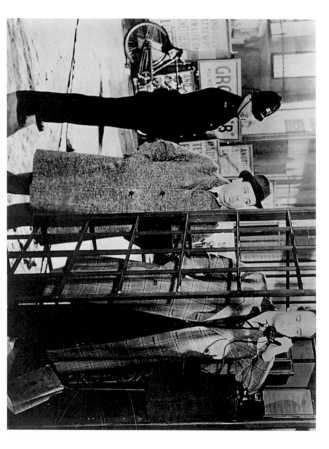

Alfred Hitchcock and George Sanders in *Rebecca*, 1940

The French poster for *Rebecca*, 1940

Robert Benchley, Joel McCrea and George Sanders in *Foreign Correspondent*, 1940

Heroines

Judith Anderson and Joan Fontaine in *Rebecca*, 1940

The American poster for *Notorious*, 1946

Eberhard Krumschmidt, Frederich Ledebur, Ivan Triesault,
Leopoldine Konstantin, Reinhold Schunzel, Peter von Zerneck, Ingrid Bergman
and Claude Rains in *Notorious*, 1946

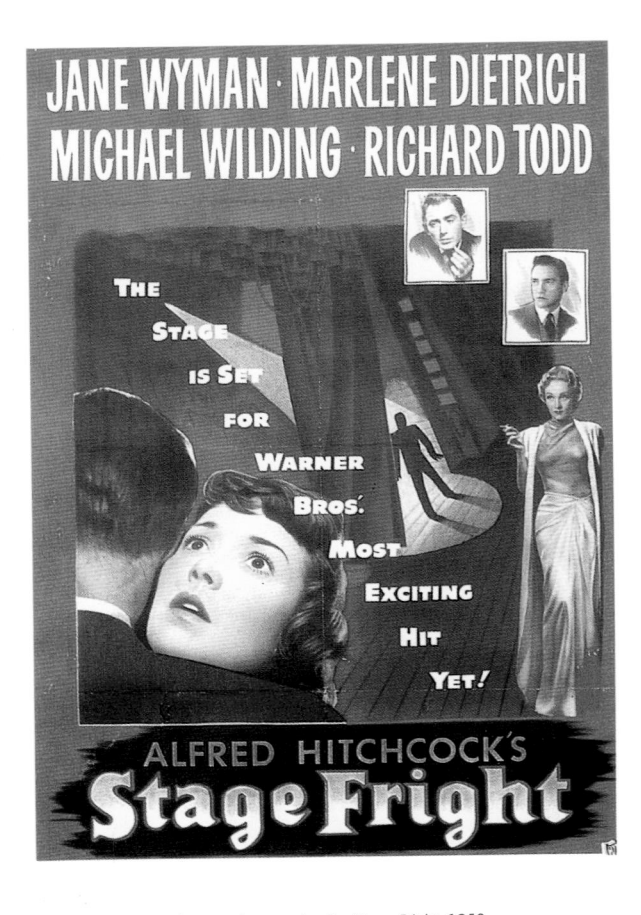

The American poster for *Stage Fright*, 1950

The Belgian poster for *Under Capricorn*, 1949

Ingrid Bergman, Joseph Cotten and Cecil Parker in *Under Capricorn*, 1949

Hitchcock with Marlene Dietrich on the set of *Stage Fright*, 1950

Hitchcock, Anne Baxter and Roger Dann during the filming of *I Confess*, 1952

World première of Hitchcock's *I Confess,* in 1953

Grace Kelly and Hitchcock during the filming of *Rear Window*, 1954

James Stewart and Grace Kelly between two scenes of *Rear Window*, 1954

Grace Kelly and James Stewart in *Rear Window*, 1954

James Stewart and Kim Novak in *Vertigo*, 1958

Janet Leigh and Hitchcock on the set of *Psycho*, 1960

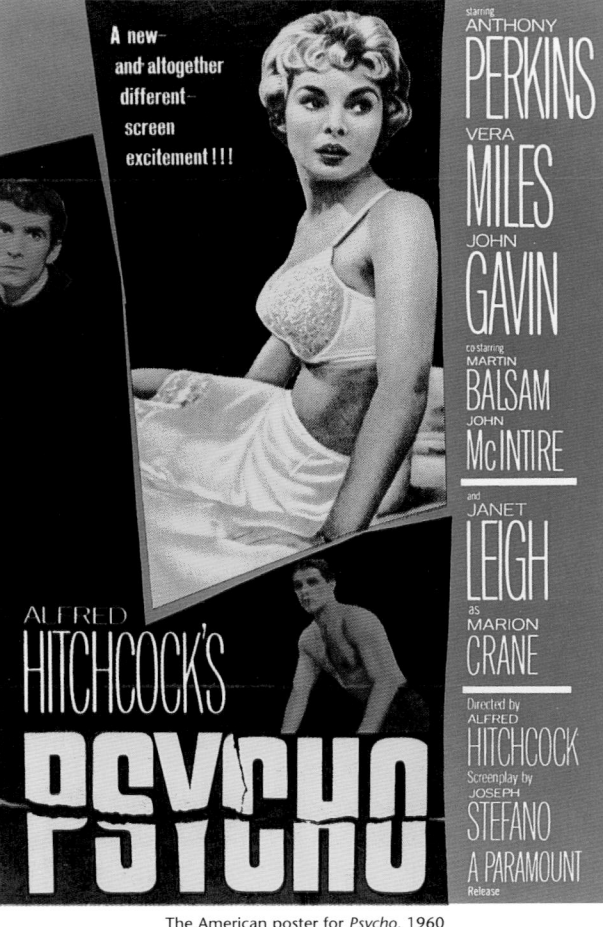

The American poster for *Psycho*, 1960

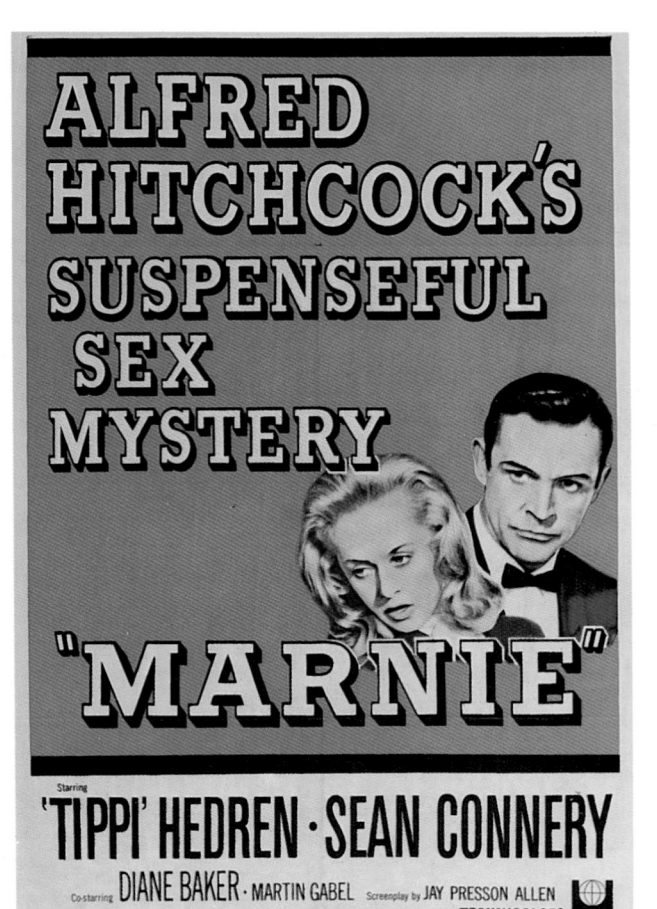

The American poster for *Marnie*, 1964

Tippi Hedren and Hitchcock during the filming of *Marnie*, 1964

Tippi Hedren and Hitchcock during the filming of *Marnie*, 1964

Hitchcock directing Julie Andrews in *Torn Curtain*, 1966

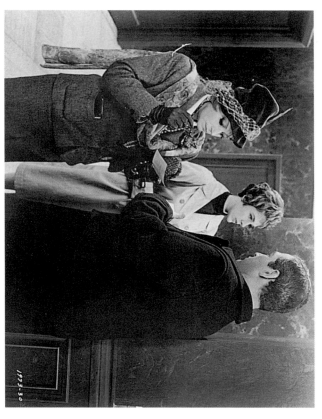

Lila Kedrova, Julie Andrews and Paul Newman in *Torn Curtain*, 1966

Great
Performers

Cary Grant, Joan Fontaine and Hitchcock on the set of *Suspicion*, 1941

The French poster for *The Paradine Case*, 1948

Hitchcock, Gregory Peck and Charles Laughton during the filming
of *The Paradine Case*, 1948

The French poster for *I Confess*, 1953

The American poster for *Rear Window*, 1954

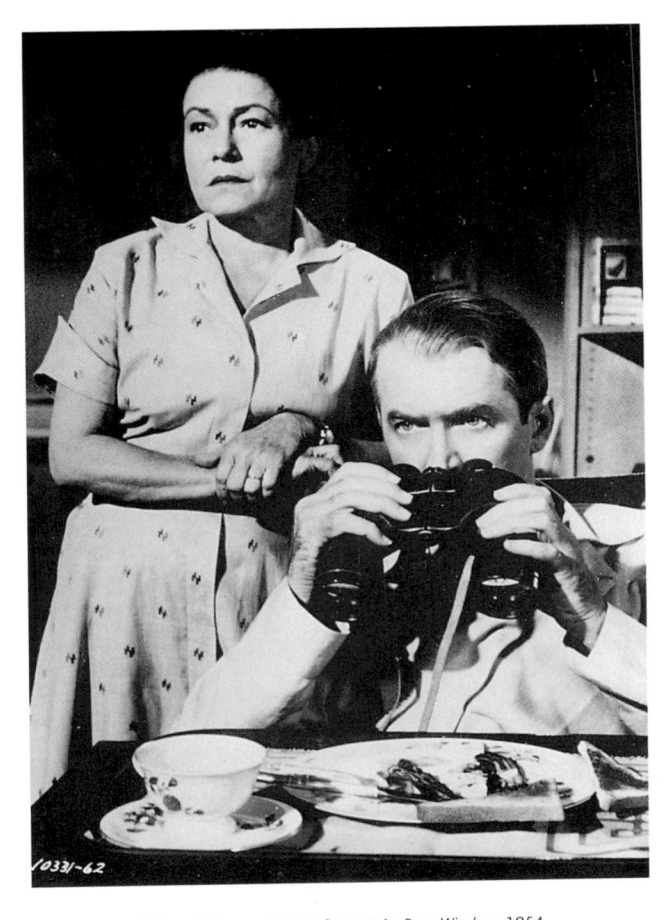

Thelma Ritter and James Stewart in *Rear Window*, 1954

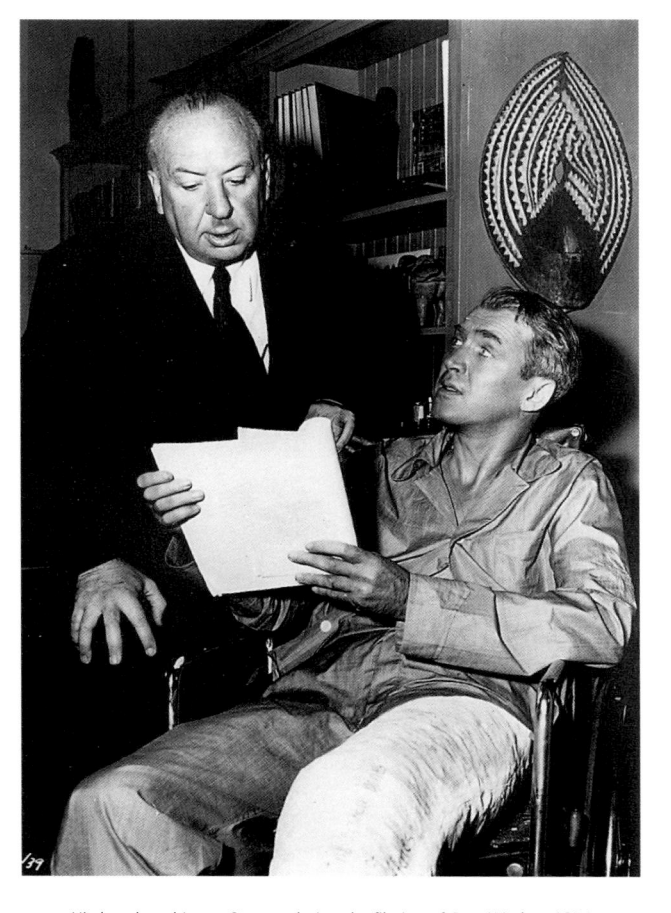

Hitchcock and James Stewart during the filming of *Rear Window*, 1954

John Williams and Cary Grant in *To Catch a Thief*, 1955

Cary Grant in *To Catch a Thief*, 1955

Cary Grant with Hitchcock on the set of *North by Northwest*, 1959

Eva Marie Saint and Cary Grant in *North by Northwest*, 1959

Anthony Perkins in *Psycho*, 1960

Anthony Perkins in *Psycho*, 1960

Hitchcock directing Sean Connery in *Marnie*, 1964

Fear

Madeleine Carroll, John Gielgud and Peter Lorre
in *The Secret Agent*, 1936

Michael Redgrave and Margaret Lockwood in *The Lady Vanishes*, 1938

Joan Fontaine and Laurence Olivier in *Rebecca*, 1940

Robert Cummings in *Saboteur*, 1942

The French poster for *Saboteur*, 1942

Joseph Cotten and Teresa Wright in *Shadow of a Doubt*, 1943

Jane Wyman, Richard Todd, Alastair Sim and Dame Sybil Thorndike in *Stage Fright*, 1950

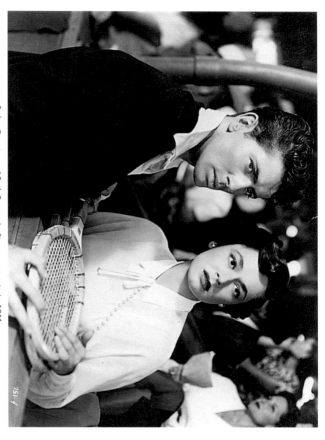

Farley Granger and Ruth Roman in *Strangers on a train*, 1951

Ray Milland in *Dial M for Murder*, 1954

Robert Cummings and Grace Kelly in *Dial M for Murder*, 1954

A scene from *Rear Window*, 1954

Grace Kelly and James Stewart in *Rear Window*, 1954

James Stewart in *Vertigo*, 1958

James Stewart in *Vertigo*, 1958

Janet Leigh and Frank Albertson in *Psycho*, 1960

Janet Leigh in *Psycho*, 1960

Anthony Perkins and Janet Leigh in *Psycho*, 1960

The American poster for *The Birds*, 1963

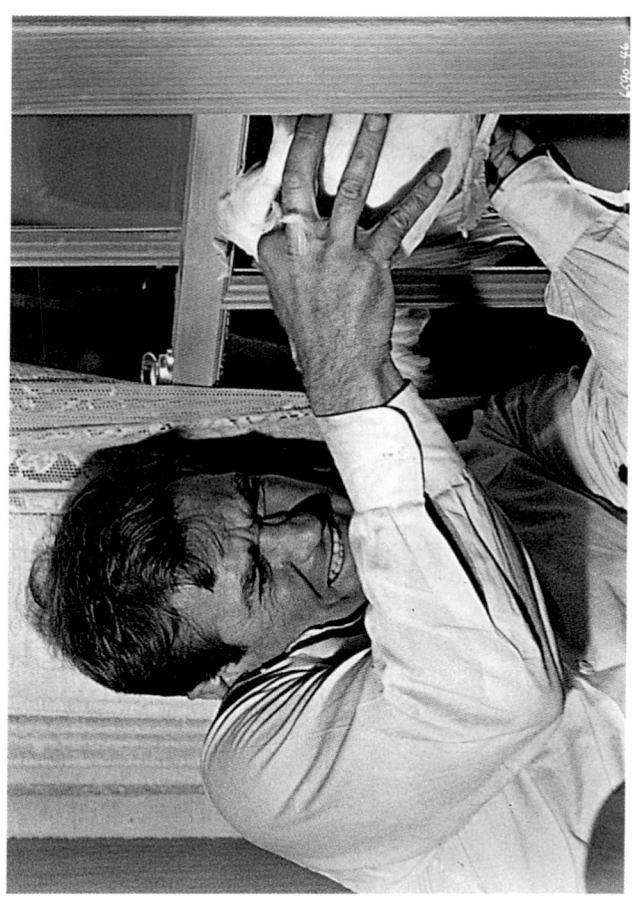

Rod Taylor in *The Birds*, 1963

Tippi Hedren in *The Birds*, 1963

Jessica Tandy, Tippi Hedren and Rod Taylor in *The Birds*, 1963

An excerpt from the storyboard of *The Birds*, 1963

Tippi Hedren and Sean Connery in *Marnie*, 1964

Tippi Hedren in *Marnie*, 1964

Romance

Norah Baring and Herbert Marshall in *Murder*, 1930

Madeleine Carroll and Robert Donat in *The 39 Steps*, 1935

The English poster for *Young and Innocent*, 1937

Derrick de Marney, Mary Clare and Nova Pilbeam in *Young and Innocent*, 1937

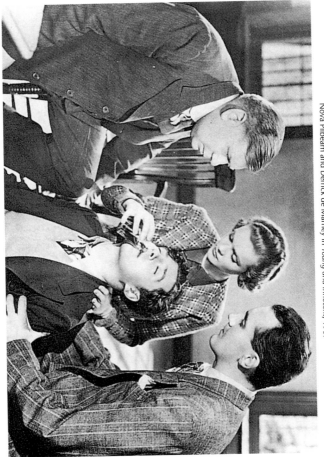

Nova Pilbeam and Derrick de Marney in *Young and Innocent*, 1937

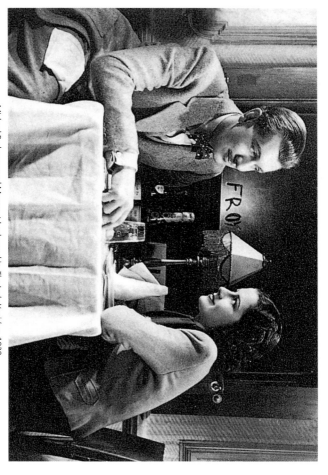

Michael Redgrave and Margaret Lockwood in *The Lady Vanishes*, 1938

Michael Redgrave, Margaret Lockwood and Paul Lukas in *The Lady Vanishes*, 1938

Michael Redgrave and Margaret Lockwood in *The Lady Vanishes*, 1938

Joan Fontaine and Laurence Olivier in *Rebecca*, 1940

Priscilla Lane and Robert Cummings in *Saboteur*, 1942

The French poster for *Spellbound*, 1945

Ingrid Bergmann and Gregory Peck in *Spellbound*, 1945

Ann Todd and Gregory Peck in *The Paradine Case*, 1948

Michael Wilding and Jane Wyman in *Stage Fright*, 1950

Farley Granger and Laura Elliott in *Strangers on a Train*, 1951

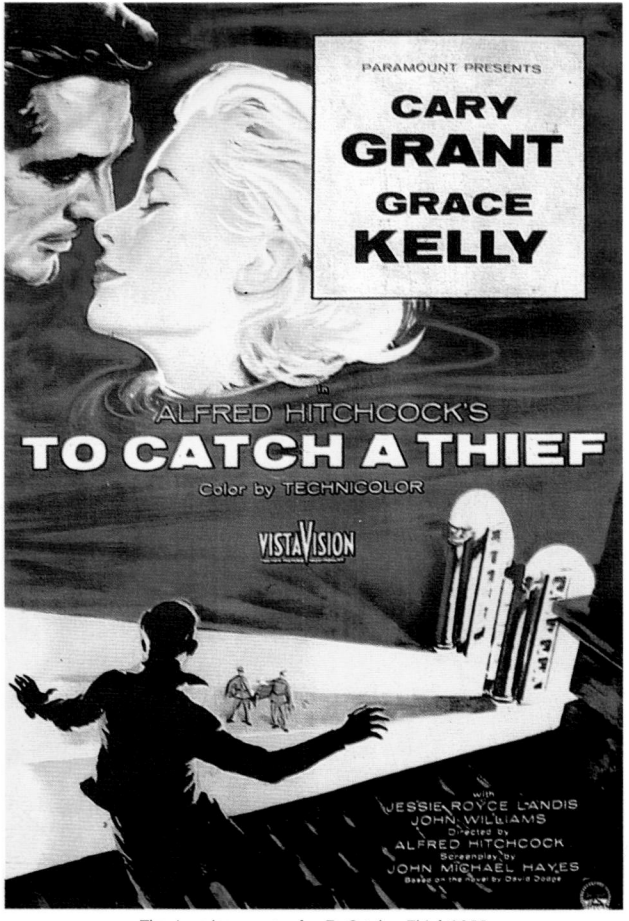

The American poster for *To Catch a Thief*, 1955

Cary Grant and Grace Kelly in *To Catch a Thief*, 1955

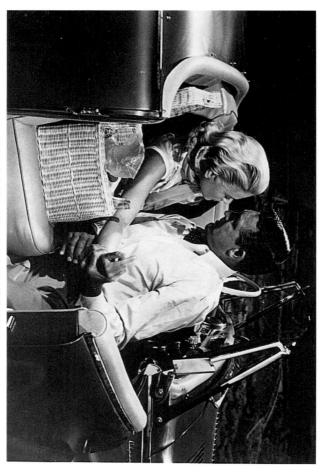

Grace Kelly and Cary Grant in *To Catch a Thief*, 1955

James Stewart and Kim Novak in *Vertigo*, 1958

Cary Grant and Eva Marie Saint in *North by Northwest*, 1959

An excerpt from the storyboard of *North by Northwest*, 1959

Janet Leigh and John Gavin in *Psycho*, 1960

John Forsythe and Claude Jade in *Topaz*, 1969

Classic
Scenes

Robert Donat in *The 39 Steps*, 1935

Naunton Wayne, Basil Radford, Linden Travers, Dame May Whitty,
Margaret Lockwood and Michael Redgrave in *The Lady Vanishes*, 1938

A key scene from *Foreign Correspondent*, 1940

Norman Lloyd and Robert Cummings in *Saboteur*, 1942

Farley Granger and James Stewart in *Rope*, 1948

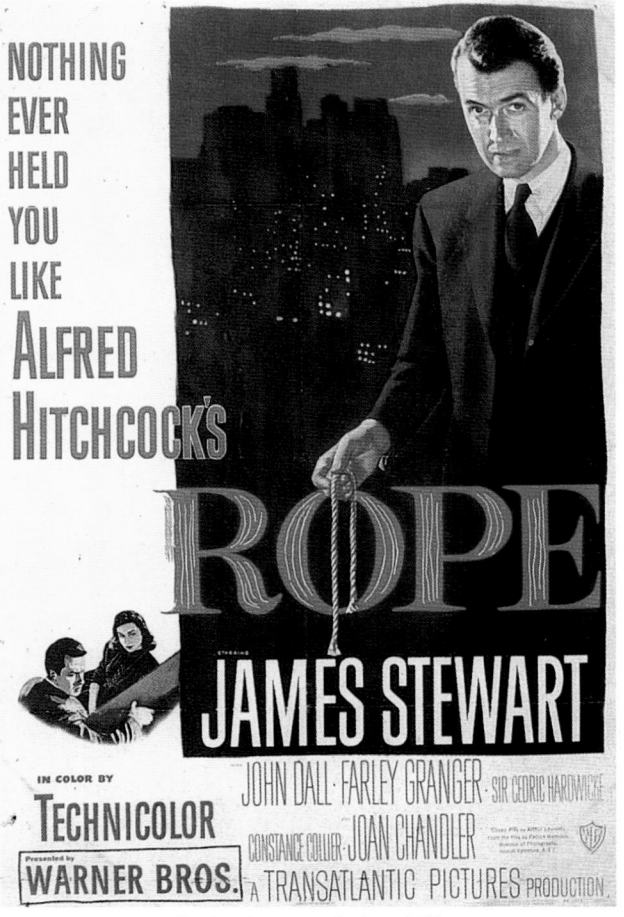

The American poster for *Rope*, 1948

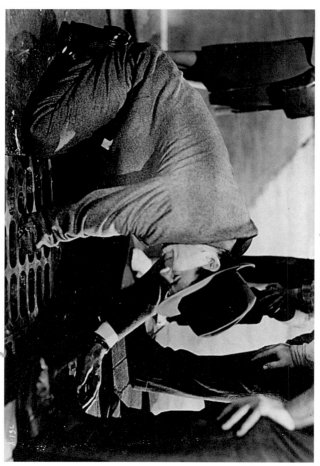

Robert Walker in *Strangers on a Train*, 1951

Farley Granger and Robert Walker in *Strangers on a Train*, 1951

Grace Kelly and Anthony Dawson in *Dial M for Murder*, 1954

Grace Kelly and Anthony Dawson in *Dial M for Murder,* 1954

James Stewart and Kim Novak in *Vertigo*, 1958

James Stewart in *Vertigo*, 1958

Cary Grant in *North by Northwest*, 1959

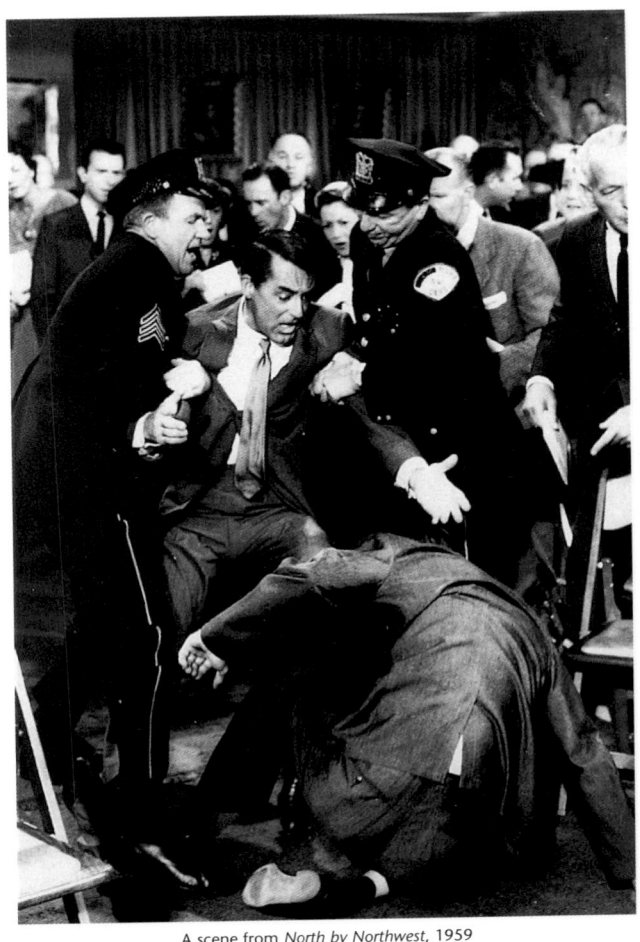

A scene from *North by Northwest*, 1959

Cary Grant in *North by Northwest*, 1959

The American poster for *North by Northwest*, 1959

Cary Grant in *North by Northwest,* 1959

A scene from *North by Northwest,* 1959

Cary Grant and Eva Marie Saint in *North by Northwest*, 1959

Cary Grant and Eva Marie Saint in *North by Northwest*, 1959

Hitchcock directing Janet Leigh in *Psycho*, 1960

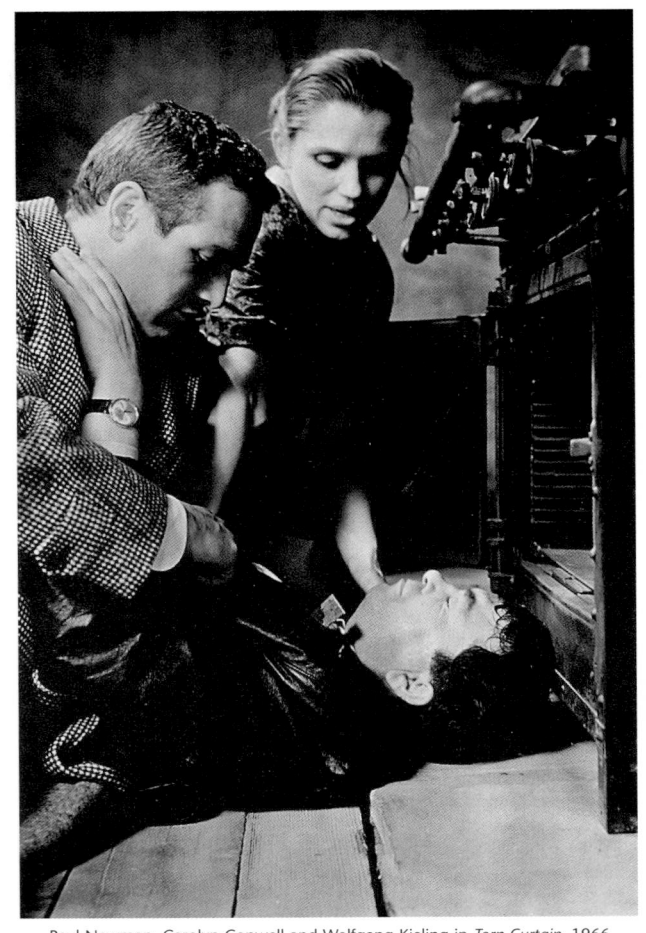

Paul Newman, Carolyn Conwell and Wolfgang Kieling in *Torn Curtain*, 1966

Hitchcock
at work

Hitchcock at work

Patricia Hitchcock with her father on the set of *Strangers on a Train*, 1951

Signing the contract for *I Confess*, 1952

Hitchcock and Roger Dann arriving in Quebec to film *I Confess*, 1952

Filming a scene of *To Catch a Thief*, 1955

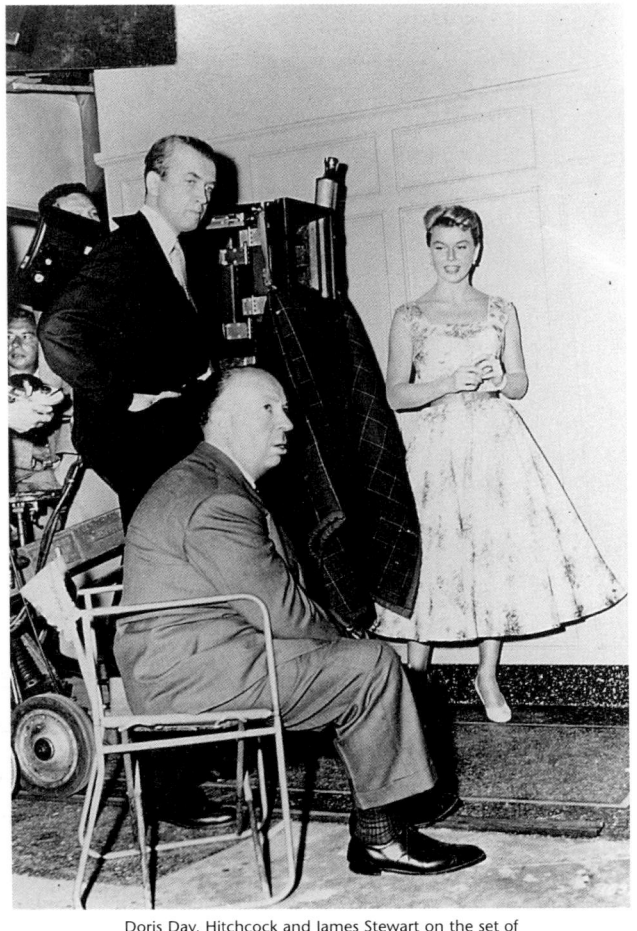

Doris Day, Hitchcock and James Stewart on the set of
The Man Who Knew too Much, 1956

Hitchcock with his family on the set of *Psycho*, 1960

Alfred Hitchcock on the set of *Family Plot*, 1976

Chronology

1926 *The Mountain Eagle; The Lodger*
1927 *Downhill; Easy Virtue; The Ring*
1928 *The Farmer's Wife; Champagne*
1929 *The Manxman; Blackmail*
1930 *Juno and the Paycock; Murder*
1931 *The Skin Game*
1932 *Rich and Strange; Number Seventeen*
1933 *Waltzes from Vienna*
1934 *The Man Who Knew Too Much*
1935 *The 39 Steps*
1936 *The Secret Agent; Sabotage*
1937 *Young and Innocent*
1938 *The Lady Vanishes*
1939 *Jamaica Inn*
1940 *Rebecca; Foreign Correspondant*
1941 *M. and Mrs. Smith; Suspicion*
1942 *Saboteur*
1943 *Shadow of a Doubt*
1944 *Lifeboat; Bon voyage* (short);
Aventure malgache (short)
1945 *Spellbound*
1946 *Notorious*
1948 *The Paradine Case; Rope*
1949 *Under Capricorn*
1950 *Stage Fright*
1951 *Strangers on a Train*
1953 *I Confess*
1954 *Dial M for Murder; Rear Window*
1955 *To Catch a Thief*
1955-1962 *TV films*

1956 *The Trouble With Harry; The Man Who Knew Too Much*
1957 *The Wrong Man*
1958 *Vertigo*
1959 *North by Northwest*
1960 *Psycho*
1963 *The Birds*
1964 *Marnie*
1966 *Torn Curtain*
1969 *Topaz*
1972 *Frenzy*
1976 *Family Plot*

Bibliography

The Dark Side of Genius
The Life of Alfred Hitchcock,
by Donald Spoto,
Little, Brown & Company

Hitchcock, by Claude Chabrol
and Éric Rohmer,
Roundhouse publications

Hitchcock, by Jean Douchet,
L'Herne

Hitchcock/Truffaut,
HarperCollins publishers